On Presence, Absence

and

Classical Hollywood Distortion

Bo Kenneth

bokenneth@outlook.de

(2003) 2019

Förlag; BoD- Books on Demand, Stockholm, Sverige

Tryck; BoD – Books on Demand, Norderstedt, Tyskland

ISBN; 978-91-7699-3897

> It is impossible for the human intellect to grasp the idea
> of absolute continuity of motion. Laws of motion of
> any kind only become comprehensible to man when he
> can examine arbitrarily selected units of that motion.
> But at the same time it is this arbitrary division of
> continuous motion into discontinuous units which gives
> rise to a large proportion of human error.
>
> Leo Tolstoy; *War and Peace*[1]

Human interaction is typically depicted in stories.

Historical annals are conspicuously stereotypical, offering organized accounts of ambiguous conflicts, accentuating the roles played by heroic heroes and vicious villains.

Or vice versa.

Out of the confusion of human coexistence historical narratives identify a patterned if paradoxical, allegedly factual yet largely fictional and illusory human universe.

A human reality.

---

[1] Tolstoy 1982, 974.

Histories of human being are remarkably irrational.

Human interaction is portrayed as an endless string of battles, in which the heroes are the villains who seem to win the wars. Where wars are fought to present and preserve heroes. And to topple villains no longer seen as heroes.

Or vice versa.

Human coexistence is seen as based on competition. On a common struggle for prosperity and presence. Where presence is inseparably linked to prosperity. And prosperity depends on possessing symbols and tokens of social presence.

Human excellence is seen as present in palatial splendour and glorious cathedrals. Built on wars and common subservience. As massive manifestations of princely power and pious sovereignty. As monuments of ceaseless struggles and insatiable greed.

Coupled with a certain sense of sumptuous glory.

+ + +

Faced with the flow of life man creates illusions.

And deities. Shaped in his image.

Aware of his transient existence, within a transient reality never completely real, man maintains a fictitious world.

In which women are offered a central if subordinate role.

Through the centuries human beings have ceaselessly reiterated stories.

In poems and sagas, novels and dramas.

Broadly sharing a narrative structure.

Through the telling of largely similar stories an integrated system of figurative configurations is repeatedly redefined.

Included in every story a narrative structure conditions the telling. While every story embodies a manifestation of a figurative world.

All stories include and redefine a recurrent scope of principles and configurations, shaped and sustained by the telling, which decisively condition the telling and constrain the scope of the story.

Infinitely variable yet structurally stable, all stories are preserved through a patterned process underpinned by a common lack of critical reflection.

+ + +

The basic principles defining and preserving a fictitious human universe are consistently, conveniently and conspicuously present in stories.

In a continuous practice of narrative regeneration.

By way of repeatedly portraying a process of self-preservation, a figurative tradition preserves itself. And continually redefining the configurations shaping the narrative conflict the narrative discourse effectively sustains a fictitious realm.

Stories underpin an endless discursive practice through which heroes and villains continually confront themselves and each other.

Offering peace through war, and freedom through subservience, a narrative discourse proposes to structure the chaos of life. And to maintain a fictitious universe.

Far from lifting the veil or breaking the spell the telling of stories sustains a narrative realm, and supports a collective illusion.

A stable network of narrative configurations dependably stimulates the telling of different yet always similar stories. In which the roles played by men and women, heroes and villains, are persistently confirmed.

+ + +

Stories are not inherently trivial.

A persistent practice of storytelling preserves a pervasive and persuasive existential strategy, in more than one respect.

Told to entertain and amuse, to explore the processes of being, stories also offer to maintain the presence of the storyteller.

Stories maintain a promise of presence.

Through a partly unconscious process of cognitive diversion.

Which is partly why stories are still being ceaselessly told.

To distinguish us from other species??

With the presence of the printing press the process of telling stories was vastly expanded.

Through commercialized film and television, a technologically assisted industrial production, of stereotypical stories, has expanded into a globalized form of massive narrative diversion and distortion.

A development significantly including a US-American component.

Thus, a kind of commercially enhanced diversion is sustained as a central discursive practice, actively promoted by a predominant proponent of a so-called Western culture.

+ + +

A human universe is deeply conditioned by stories.

And by an endless line of heroes, assumed to command the course of a common struggle. To preserve a promise of presence and power, through solving conflicts broadly caused by the struggle.

Within a human universe heroes have to struggle to sustain their presence.

And their powers.

Through arousing and sustaining the angst required to sustain the struggles aimed at alleviating the angst.

Where heroes are seldom seen as embodiments of angst and irrationality.

A human universe embraces an illusory realm.

As suggested by widespread celebration of heroes and idols. Sustained through deceptive rituals and practices. Which include and redefine a broadly self-deceptive mode of being.

In which most aspects are consistently distorted and perverted.

A reversed reality.

Turned upside down.

+ + +

A human universe may be seen as a deeply flawed and fallacious realm.

In spite of claims as to human rationality and ingenuity.

In spite of continuous efforts aimed at verifying and substantiating the absolute existence of an objectified reality.

By way of assumed and presupposed abstractions and axioms.

By way dogma and doctrines. Sustained by experiential evidence.

And linguistic figuration.

A human universe is partly maintained through a ceaseless practice of reiterating stories.

Redefining and consolidating a fictitious realm. Frequently seen as real.

While obscuring the underlying complexity conditioning the continuity of figurative regeneration.

An essentially primitive and still primeval human universe is persistently redefined through a partly blind and unconscious discursive interplay. Veiled and obscured by illusory presence.

By an irrational reality.

Involving an integrated practice of figurative interaction and regeneration, the classical Hollywood drama embodies and illustrates the dynamics of discursive diversion.

Of visual and verbal re-presentation.

And narrative distortion.

Conspicuously visual the Hollywood film includes and illuminates a regenerative interplay.

Enhanced by verbal and conceptual presence.

While often considered a technical accessory, a scaffolding to be removed once the film is made, the Hollywood screenplay identifies an integrated network of transparent verbal and conceptual configurations.

Simultaneously stimulating and restraining the regeneration of the visual presence.

Whereas an image may speak more than a thousand words, words and images are inherently illusory.

While a continuous flow of moving pictures persuasively portrays a seemingly real fictitious world, a ceaseless discursive practice is fundamental to maintain the figurative configurations sustaining the illusion of reality.

It is beyond the power of the human intellect to
encompass *all* the causes of any phenomenon. But the
impulse to search into causes is inherent in man's very
nature. And so the human intellect, without
investigating the multiplicity and complexity of
circumstances conditioning an event, any one of which
taken separately may seem to be the reason for it,
snatches at the first most comprehensible approximation
to a cause and says; 'There is the cause!'

Leo Tolstoy; *War and Peace*[2]

In *Der Sichtbare Mensch*, written in 1923, librettist, filmmaker and early
film theorist Béla Balázs welcomes the return of a visual culture[3].

Similar to the printing press a new machine is seen to
inaugurate an altered cultural direction. And to shift a collective attention
back from a culture of concepts, which "gradually rendered illegible the
faces of men".

Like the printing press the new machine offers to enhance "the
multiplication and distribution of products of the human spirit", where the
cinematographic camera seems to renew "the rich and colourful language
of gesture, movement and facial expression".

To renew a culture in which "Man has again become visible".

---

[2] Tolstoy 1982, 1168.
[3] Balázs 1972, 39ff.

15

In Balázs' inspired account the machine is identified as a basic causal agent prompting a new process of development and change.

With the subsequent introduction of sound, however, this process later brought back a significant verbal and conceptual presence.

To A.R. Fulton, writing with the advantage of hindsight, motion pictures, "the newest of the arts, the only art to originate in the twentieth century, are a product of the Machine Age"[4].

Motion pictures are seen to depend "to a greater extent than any other art, upon machinery", and the cinematic machine, described as "the machinery that makes the pictures, and that makes them motion pictures", embraces the complex apparatus employed to operate and control production, distribution and exhibition.

In Fulton's discussion the focus is shifted from the machine to the movement of the machine.

And further to the processes of trial and error, innovation and development behind the appearance of the overall apparatus.

The origin of motion pictures is linked to the pragmatic "ingenuity and effort, not of artists, but of inventors, mechanics, photographers, engineers and manufacturers", whose utilitarian purpose was "to perfect a machine that would have a use".

Commercial and financial problems and prospects came to equal and rival technical considerations, and Thomas Edison presents an example of "an inventor aware of the importance of patents on devices that could be manufactured for profit".

Thus including a wider causal scope Fulton concludes that "The essential principles of motion picture photography and projection

---

[4] Fulton 1985, 27ff.

having at last been applied in a commercial enterprise, motion pictures were born" (38).

On the basis of what he calls a "neoclassical economic theory of technical change" Douglas Gomery distinguishes between the phases of invention, innovation and diffusion, through which a commercial enterprise actively explores, develops and disseminates new products or processes for the purpose of commercial gain[5].

Through the combined efforts of individual entrepreneurs and industrial enterprises invention is followed by innovation as the implementation of technological change to obtain and secure a financial yield.

Industrial corporations will typically formulate their decisions "with a view toward maximizing long-run profits", and according to Gomery such motivation "propelled the American motion picture industry (as it had other industries) into a new era of growth and prosperity" (234).

Coupled with commercial motivation the prospect of individual financial compensation, and subsequent social recognition, may seem pivotal to the invention, production and promotion of motion pictures.

Both Fulton and Gomery accentuate the aggressive involvement of the individual inventor or entrepreneur, of "these men – from Muybridge with his pictures of Leland Stanford's horses to Edison with his Vitascope".

Also recognizing a financial aspect as well as a personal perspective, Stephen Heath observes that "Lumière and even Edison in this field, to take the two habitual 'founders' of cinema, were exploiters and businessmen, developers rather than inventors"[6].

---

[5] Gomery 1985A, 229ff.
[6] Heath 1981, 227.

17

In a similar discussion Raymond Williams addresses the rapid expansion of television.

Of another machine seen to further a visual culture, and at a time considered to foster radical cultural change.

Williams notes that technology is often viewed as "a self-acting force", active within an independent or marginal sphere, with a capacity to create or provide the basis for "new societies or new human conditions", for "new ways of life"[7].

In view of an aspect of intention inherent in processes of research and development, rather than deterministic or "symptomatic" and a by-product of a social practice, technology may be regarded as "direct" and resulting from "known social needs, purposes and practices to which the technology is not marginal but central"[8].

Analogous to the Hollywood cinema television emerged through a competitive rivalry between different systems and commercially motivated organizations. Between individually motivated and collectively organized men, and a few women. The machinery required for television broadcasting may thus be seen as "the applied technology of a set of emphases and responses within the determining limits and pressures of industrialist capitalist society" (27).

Also concerned with "the force of the isolation of technology" in historical accounts, Heath expands Williams' discussion, and refers to "the process of cinema" as "a process through which in particular economic situations a set of scattered technical devices becomes an applied technology then a fully social technology" (221).

---

[7] Cited in Heath 1981, 225-226.
[8] Williams 1990, 14ff.

In lieu of a history of technological invention "with questions of understanding collapsed into the mechanical assertion of chains of cause and effect", Heath proposes a history of "a multiply determined development, a process" which is "a history of the technological and social together, a history in which the determinations are not simple but multiple, interacting" (227).

And later modifying the role played by the machine Balázs recognizes an expanded causal scope; "it was not by accident that [the technique of cinematography] emerged at the time when other intellectual products were also beginning to be produced on a large industrial scale [...] The wholesale industrialization of art and literature did not start with the film, but the film arrived when this trend was just gathering momentum" (23).

+ + +

Whereas the process of cinema involves and depends on the machine, the cinematic apparatus is only maintained by the movement of the machine.

By motion pictures.

The apparatus embraces the process, and the process is manifest in a machine or apparatus which embodies both cause and effect, as the result of an open-ended interplay in which everything is related to everything else.

Rather than the cinematic apparatus or machinery, however, the visual presence will appear as the most conspicuous manifestation of an integrated process, which includes a crucial element of feedback.

In which transparent causal aspects are masked by the presence, and obscured by the complexity of the all-embracing interaction.

19

Instead, "emergent regularities" may signal the prospect of regenerative patterns and configurations which, simultaneously characterize and condition the presence and the process.

Masked by the visual presence the process involves and depends on a patterned and systemic interplay, which identifies and incorporates the generative and regulative relational configurations shaping the process and sustaining the presence[9].

+ + +

David Bordwell shows how a set of conventionalized devices, systems and systemic relations distinguish and define "a style whose principles remain quite constant across decades, genres, studios, and personnel"[10].

Rather than a geographically determined category the so-called classical Hollywood style identifies a unified system of "integral and limited stylistic conventions", which at the same time impose "stringent limits on individual innovation", while constituting "a fairly coherent aesthetic tradition which sustains individual creation".

Individually distinguishable in consequence to a certain creative diversity Hollywood films remain conspicuously uniform, where a classical and conservative aspect may be seen to support the vitality of the tradition.

What André Bazin describes as "the genius of the system"[11].

A predefined systemic configuration, identified by the classical style, is repeatedly redefined by the film performance.

---

[9] This dynamic model is further described in Varela 1993; Goertzel 1994; and Capra 1997.
[10] Bordwell 1994, 3ff.
[11] Cited in ibid, 4.

The visual performance includes and illustrates a regenerative process conditioned by principles and patterns continually consolidated through the process.

In terms of systemic regenerative configurations the classical style identifies what Bordwell describes as "an underlying logic which is not apparent from our common-sense reflections upon the films", but which "like Poe's purloined letter, 'escapes observation by dint of being excessively obvious'" (11)

The more or less logical configurations suggested by the classical Hollywood style are also described and discussed in numerous textbooks on practical screenwriting.

To some extent visualized in the film performance conventionalized stylistic and generic configurations also include significant verbal and conceptual, mythical and metaphysical elements, which are readily recognizable in the standardized and paradigmatic Hollywood screenplay.

Illustrating the shift signalled by the visual culture, the verbal aspect of the Hollywood film is seldom explicitly addressed.

In spite of the added discursive force offered by the introduction of sound, through which music and aural scenography decisively enhance an integrated visual and verbal interplay, non-visual features are typically assumed as self-evident elements of a more pressing visual presence.

Mostly overshadowed by a conspicuous visual performance, more transparent verbal and conceptual principles and configurations are distinctly specified and described in the frequently overlooked screenplay.

In the Hollywood drama.

In 1943 John Gassner, introducing the first volume of *Twenty Best Film Plays*, optimistically announces that "There is now a new literature of the screen – the screenplay. If this fact has not been widely recognized, it is only because screenplays have not been properly accorded the dignity of print"[12].

Nearly a decade later, Balázs describes the film script as "an entirely new literary form, newer even than the film itself, and so it is scarcely surprising that no books on the aesthetics of literature mention it as yet" (246).

While "the Philistines" were initially reluctant to accept the film as "an independent, autonomous new art with laws of its own", Balázs confidently concludes that "To-day this is scarcely ever questioned and it is also admitted that the literary foundation of the new art, the script, is just as much a specific, independent literary form as the written stage play".

Also writing in 1952 Williams argues that although "today a [stage] play is hardly considered to be a literary form", the development of the prose play from 1850 to 1950, from Ibsen to Eliot, must lead to the conclusion that "drama is essentially a literary form, but a literary form which requires, for its communication, all the technical elements of performance"[13].

Williams views the theatrical performance as "the means of communication of dramatic literature", where literature in turn is seen as

---

[12] Gassner 1943.
[13] Williams 1964, 16ff.

"a form of communication of imaginative experience through certain written organizations of words".

In the naturalist prose drama the role played by language is modified in relation to the characters and the action "in such a way as to make it appear not to exist at all" (24). A consequent linguistic transparency, described as "this change of the conventional level of language", employed for the purpose of creating "the illusion of reality", is viewed by Williams as the "principal modification which naturalism effected in the drama" (25).

Dramatic naturalism hence suggests an accentuation of characters and action to the extent that the characters may be considered as "absolute", and it is "the fact that these parts become apparently independent, in the flesh-and-blood illusion of the dramatic performance, which has so often misled dramatic criticism" (21).

Contrary to a theatrical performance, in which visual scenography often forms "a mere background", the film is seen by Balázs to project all its elements "on to the same plane", and the screenwriter has to include "the part played by the images of things every bit as carefully as all the other parts", in a balanced accordance with other dramatic, stylistic and literary elements (249).

Other distinguishing features include a particular kind of visual writing, involving specific devices such as sudden cuts, close-ups and constantly shifting points of view.

As a result, the film medium employs and enjoys visual strategies and an expressive visual form-language which are different from the traditional stage play.

A visual emphasis is also seen in the prudent or "poetic" facet of screenwriting, and to George Garrett "It is possible that poets would make the best screenwriters"[14].

Similarly, in Balázs' opinion the film script presents "a literary form worthy of the pen of the poets" (246).

Syd Field pragmatically insists that all screenplays seriously considered for costly productions include a certain conceptual framework, ordered in a basic linear structure and constituting what both Field and Bordwell label a "paradigm"[15].

Like Bordwell Field outlines the recurring features of a narrative structure, an integrated configuration viewed by Douglas Garrett Winston as "the best known and most influential form of the narrative screenplay"[16].

Apart from stylistic features and elements of cinematic form-language a typical Hollywood screenplay includes an Aristotelian structure.

In addition to a beginning, a middle and an end designed to attract and sustain attention, William Goldman identifies a number of considerations which to varying degrees stimulate and restrain the practice of screenwriting, such as financial requirements, popular trends and concerns towards "protecting the star" [17].

The most decisive factor, however, acknowledged by most if not all screenwriters, is to tell a good story well.

+ + +

---

[14] Garrett 1967, 111.
[15] Field 1984, 7-8.
[16] Winston 1973, 64.
[17] Goldman 1984, 129.

David Howard and Edward Mabley isolate the two predominant concerns of the filmmaker as how to develop a good story, and how to tell it well[18].

The screenwriter and the director are seen as "the only two people involved in a film production who look at the film in nearly the same way; the totality of the story; how it is told; how an audience will experience it and react to it".

Prescriptive guidelines as to a stringent plot-pattern and a limited number of pages suggest a standardized form employed for the purpose of telling a well-defined story within a predefined temporal span.

With reference to the sonnet and the short story Balázs confirms that "The theme, content and style of the film script must be inspired by the predetermined length of it. This predetermined length is in itself a style which the script-writer must master" (255).

Balázs interestingly sees the interplay of form and content in commercial filmmaking as temporarily settled into a stable condition. Thus, "once the river bed is made it collects the waters of the surrounding countryside and gives them shape" (257).

The form shapes the content until a "mighty flood" may change the course of the river.

Together, the customs and conventions, the classical style and the form-language support a cinema of narrative integration which according to Tom Gunning "subordinates film form to the development of stories and characters", where a process of "narrativization" facilitates the transformation of showing into telling[19].

Introduced by Heath the concept describes the integration and unification of the film performance, the welding together of "screen and frame, ground and background, surface and depth, the whole setting of

---

[18] Howard 1993, 14ff.
[19] Gunning 1994, 6ff.

movements and transitions, the implication of space and spectator in the taking place of film as narrative"[20].

With the process of narrativization the film achieves its "organic unity", within a coherent "narrative space" ideally without gaps or contradictions, and including an essential subjective element.

To Gunning narrativization adds a fourth aspect to Gerard Genette's triad of story, discourse and the act of narrating, as a process that "binds narrative discourse to story and rules the narrator's address to the spectator" (16).

The effect of the process is that of "carving a story out of a photographic reality".

A photographic reality, one might add, which is deeply deceptive and illusory.

$+++$

The presence of the story may seem to obscure the practice of telling.

Conspicuously visual, the process of narrativization also integrates and incorporates a broad range of generative and regulative configurations identified by a mythical and metaphysical framework.

Obviously conditioned by the story, and by the narrative structure, the practice of telling embraces a significant if transparent conceptual aspect, and in addition to stylistic principles and a cinematic form-language, the Hollywood screenplay includes and depends on a systemic verbal interplay.

In what he fears may sound like a tautology Andrew Kennedy argues that "The governing concept for all dramatic dialogue is *verbal interaction*"[21].

---

[20] Heath 1982, 43.
[21] Kennedy 1983, 2ff.

In one of very few studies of dramatic dialogue Kennedy points to the rich network of ideas behind the Greek word "*dialogos*", where the term at least should recapture "an echo of the Greek significance of *logos* – one of the keywords of Western culture, connecting word and meaning, language and reality".

Supported by Peter Szondi's study of the post-Renaissance drama, in which "interpersonal relations have a unique role in defining and reflecting the condition of man – man in the sphere of 'between'", Kennedy views all types of dramatic dialogue "from stichomythia through blank verse to naturalistic prose – [as] embraced and illuminated by the interactive concept" (8).

Including processes of verbal interaction, the Hollywood screenplay embraces and illuminates a regenerative linguistic interplay.

Which redefines and integrates the conceptual configurations underpinning the mythical and metaphysical fabric supporting the narrative structure.

And hence the style, the form-language and the process of narrativization.

In a network of regenerative interaction.

Ferdinand de Saussure defines a language as "a system of signs expressing ideas", where a linguistic sign is described as "a two-sided psychological entity" which is "connected in the brain by an associative link"[22].

The sign does not signal "a link between a thing and a name, but between a concept and a sound pattern", labelled a "signified" and a "signifier". And whereas a sound may suggest "something physical", the sound pattern is "the hearer's psychological impression of a sound".

---

[22] Saussure 1983, 8ff.

Mentally unified signs, like all linguistic phenomena, "always present two complementary facets, each depending on the other", and the "positive" presence suggested by signs and ideas rests on an interplay of difference which at the same time separates and associates individually inadequate and unproductive signifiers and signifieds.

Saussure significantly observes that "in language there are only differences", and whereas "a difference generally implies positive terms between which the difference is set up […] in language there are only differences *without positive terms*".

The relationships linking signifiers and signifieds are strictly arbitrary and based on collective habits and conventions, institutionalized through a continuous linguistic discourse.

Emerging through the discourse the presence of the sign includes a regenerative discourse as well as the relational networks simultaneously identified by and stimulating the discourse.

Beyond the signifier and the signified, the interplay of linguistic regeneration embraces and depends on a systemic network of relational interdependence included in and identifying an extensive and comprehensive interactive space describable as a "discursive field".

While recognizable as dualistic configurations of so-called binary oppositions, a far more complex relational interplay includes and integrates structures of difference at different levels, usually if somewhat inaccurately described in "positive" terms as presence.

At any level, linguistic presence embodies an underlying interplay in which networks of difference identify and express the generative and regulative "energies" underpinning and maintaining the presence and the process.

Similarly suggesting a positive term the idea of linguistic energy is based on the reciprocal influence or interdependence linking and separating configurations of difference at different levels.

Recognizable in terms of logic and grammar, style and form, discursive energies simultaneously stimulating and regulating the discourse are always inherent in linguistic presence, in linguistic meaning.

Embodied in the meaning these energies are expressed through the interplay of discursive responses conditioned by and regenerating the meaning.

A theoretically inexhaustible discursive potential is thus maintained through the cyclical processes of linguistic regeneration.

At the same time present and transparent, manifestations of meaning emerge from, embody and stimulate the discourse, within a "closed" yet all-inclusive interplay of systemic cyclical regeneration, a largely self-regulative interplay without apparent beginning or end.

Embracing integrated networks of signs and ideas, configurations of meaning may be seen as systemic and always variable linguistic attractors, or networks of attractors, describable as regenerative manifestations of continuous discursive processes[23].

The meaning conditions the discourse, and the practice of telling is compelled and constrained by the tale.

An interplay of parts is inherent in the whole, and Kennedy observes that "Behind the immediate dialogue sequence lies the totality of the play and its language; the gradual build-up of action, the whole network of motifs, phrases, words repeated till they become keywords –

[23] See Gleick 1990, 133ff.

in short, the complex overall dialogue 'behind' each particular dialogue"[24].

Always stimulated and restrained by the story, the Hollywood drama is repeatedly regenerated through a process which includes a linguistically conditioned and subjectively dependent interplay.

+ + +

A dramatic dialogue is inherently directed towards an "anonymous and non-conversational auditor/spectator"[25].

A dramatic discourse always assumes and employs a flux of different and shifting subjective perspectives, defined through an extended dialogical interplay.

Identified by Emile Benveniste as the subject of speech, the speaking and the spoken subject, the roles played by different and interdependent subjective manifestations are underlined by Kaja Silverman, who argues "that signification occurs only through discourse, that discourse requires a subject, and that the subject itself is an effect of discourse"[26].

Benveniste views language, discourse and subjectivity are theoretically inseparable, with "the pronouns 'I' and 'you' as signifiers which are only capable of signifying in concrete discursive situations – as signifiers without conventional signifieds" (43).

The presence of the subject is only sustained through a continuous regenerative process which in turn depends on an interplay of fluctuating yet integrated subjective perspectives.

---

[24] Kennedy 1983, 10.
[25] Ibid., 11.
[26] Silverman 1984, vii.

Present in every perspective the subject conditions and constrains the scope of the play and hence the presence.

Inherent in every aspect of presence, a transparent subject embodies a relative and self-referential attractor, in relation to which presence and difference are "re-cognized" and regenerated.

Albert Einstein has shown how three-dimensional presence includes and identifies time as a transparent fourth dimension.

This dimension vastly expands an interactive cosmic space, and identifies a theoretically infinite space-time continuum.

Similarly, manifestations of spatio-temporal subjective presence anticipate and postulate an obvious if equally transparent cognitive dimension.

Again, an all-inclusive interactive space is further widened and deepened to include absence as well as presence, the unconscious as well as conscious awareness.

A never completely present subject is hence located within and "beyond" an infinite experiential realm, as part of and apart from a subjectively defined if culturally conditioned experiential reality.

+ + +

Presence is essentially re-cognized and regenerated as cognitive experience.

Experiential presence emerges through a ceaseless interplay of shifting subjective perspectives, and an overall experiential space is continually redefined through conscious and unconscious responses conditioned by subjective re-cognition of simultaneously regenerated presence, difference and absence, always ordered and structured in relation to a persistently redefined experiential subject.

31

Within and beyond a subjectively defined and culturally specific experiential universe everything is identified in terms of presence, difference and absence, where a basic difference separating and associating subjective presence and absence is seen to constitute an essential relational configuration.

As exemplified by linguistic signification the systemic relational configurations shaping and sustaining an experiential interplay are identified, conventionalized and consolidated through the continuous process.

Significantly, Saussure observes that "Whether we take the signified or the signifier, language has neither ideas or sounds that existed before the linguistic system but only conceptual and phonic differences that have issued from the system"[27].

Stimulated by generative patterns, and balanced by regulative rules, the process incorporates and redefines a network of essentially arbitrary configurations, institutionalized through the cyclical regeneration of culturally specific experiential realities.

Contrary to the rigid rules of simple static systems, the "composionality" offered by experiential regeneration signals a significant aspect of probability, expressed through intrinsic variation and a latent "disruptive" potential, both distinguishing a dynamic interplay.

In consequence to an immense relational complexity, coupled with a decisive element of feedback and a pivotal play of shifting subjective perspectives, a continuous process of experiential regeneration is infinitely variable.

---

[27] Saussure, cited in Silverman 1984, 9.

"Closed" in the sense of being self-referential, the cyclical play includes and depends on a crucial element of variation, which supports a regenerative rather than reproductive process.

+ + +

A standardized but never identical Hollywood drama depends on and illustrates a stable yet always changing interplay of experiential regeneration, where more or less creative variations and imaginative modifications serve to enhance the regenerative energy.

Variations occur almost exclusively at the level of detail, and Bordwell notes that "Across history, the paradigm develops chiefly through changes in the first level of analysis – that of devices" (7).

Recognizable in terms of difference, variations add to a regenerative potential which is curbed by the controlling momentum of the paradigm, where opposite "forces" will seem to preserve and express the vitality if not the genius of the Hollywood system.

A continuous discursive process , which never completely repeats itself, may temporarily confirm the presence but never conclusively "close" the interplay.

Instead of a linear transfer of a clearly defined and conclusively communicated story, the processes of narrative regeneration are conditioned but not determined by simplified and incomplete discursive principles and patterns, consciously and unconsciously re-cognized throughout the discourse.

Always re-cognized from shifting and only partly shared subjective perspectives, the interplay supports the regeneration of plausible and probable yet inconclusive and never absolutely present mythical and metaphysical configurations.

33

While broadly predictable, successive re-presentations of mythical dramatic presence are never identical, even when observed from integrated subjective perspectives.

To Keir Elam dramatic worlds are constructed "from within", shown through self-referential processes, without narrative mediation, and "revealed through the persons, actions and statements which make them up"[28].

Dramatic actualization involves a mimetic rather than diegetic mode of representation, a "reflexive" process of direct imitation instead of narrative description.

As opposed to an imaginary elsewhere, describable as "there and then", a spatio-temporal "here and now" is identified as hypothetically actual, with verbal indices and deictic definitions as crucial markers of the present context.

According to Elam the founding principle of dramatic representation is "the fiction of the *presence* of a world known to be hypothetical" (112).

Emerging through the discourse a transient dramatic presence incorporates a generic structure as well as a non-linear, heterogeneous, discontinuous and incomplete interplay regenerating and integrating a dramatic world (119).

At the same time, dramatic presence effectively masks and obscures the underlying configurations shaping the discourse and sustaining the presence.

---

[28] Elam 1993, 110-114.

Bordwell discusses the justifying and unifying aspects of the Hollywood narrative in terms of causality and motivation; "Understanding classical story causality takes us toward grasping how a classical film unifies itself", where "Generally speaking, this unity is a matter of *motivation*"[29].

Motivation is described as "the process by which a narrative justifies its story material and the plot's presentation of that story material", with "compositional" motivation seen as supported by and overriding realistic and intertextual, generic and artistic motivational features.

Compositional motivation embraces interrelated systems of classical spatial, temporal and causal relations, and the individual film is seen to present "an instance of the overall dynamics of cause and effect" (17).

Character-centred causality provides "the armature of the classical story", and "Psychological causality, presented through defined characters acting to achieve announced goals, gives the classical film its characteristic progression".

With reference to Ferdinand Brunetière's dictum describing "the central law of the drama [as] that of conflict arising from obstacles to the character's desire", Bordwell argues that "Once defined as an individual through traits and motifs, the character assumes a causal role because of his or her desires" (16).

Responding in accordance with more or less articulated motifs and desires, the central character will seem to spur the action and maintain the movement, where Frederick Palmer distinguishes between "merely motion" and "the outward expression of inner feelings"[30].

---

[29] Bordwell 1994, 12ff.
[30] Cited in ibid., 15.

Figurative verisimilitude "usually supports compositional motivation by making the chain of causality seem plausible", and Bordwell refers to Francis Marion who relates the cinematic illusion of reality to tight causal motivation (19).

At the same time, compositional motivation commonly outweighs realistic motivation; "Hollywood's use of Freudian psychology was highly selective and distorting, trimming and thinning psychoanalytical concepts to fit an existing model of clear characterization and causality" (21).

The central character will to a considerable extent appear to embody and express the energy inherent in the Hollywood drama.

The unfolding of the story is inseparably linked to the early appearance and presence of the hero, who is defined through what Elam sees as an asymmetric "floor-apportionment control"[31], as a readily identifiable focus of attention and attraction.

As a principal regenerative agent a largely predefined and discursively redefined hero simultaneously emerges from and stimulates a subject-centred interplay, identifying an interdependent and "self"-referential attractor at the heart of an ordered, structured and apparently closed dramatic world.

Goldman declares that there is "no single more important commercial element in screenplay writing than the star part"[32].

To Ken Dancyger and Jeff Rush the central character represents "the primary means for the audience to experience the story"[33].

---

[31] Elam 1993, 181.
[32] Goldman 1984, 129.
[33] Dancyger 1995, 4.

Related to dramatic writing in general, Lajos Egri views "human character, in all its infinite ramifications and dialectical contradictions", as the force "which will unify all parts, a force out of which they will grow as naturally as limbs grow from the body"[34].

The hero will thus seem to embody the structural and relational nucleus of the dramatic world, with the unfolding of the story depending on his sustained presence, and with all other parts and characters, with the possible exception of the heroine, forming a properly labelled background.

As much as the hero, however, the difference separating and inseparably linking the hero and the background identifies a fundamental regenerative force.

From a position within and apart from the rest of the setting the hero's responses arise from a crucial relational configuration distinguishing presence from absence.

+ + +

Frank Daniel, echoing Brunetière's dictum, describes the constitutive principle of cinematic storytelling as; "Somebody wants something badly and is having difficulty getting it"[35].

Bordwell similarly views Hollywood characters, and particularly protagonists, as distinctly goal-oriented; "The hero desires something new to his/her situation, or the hero seeks to restore an original state of affairs"(16).

These observations relate the causal and motivational potential expressed by the hero to something that is missing and hence absent, but

---

[34] Egri 1960, xvi.
[35] Cited in Howard, 1993, xii.

at the same time present as a desire, and objectified in the form of a recognizable goal.

The narrative conflict, typically related to the presence of obstacles and difficulties, characteristically depends on the presence of absence.

+ + +

While the absence of money, love or an original condition may seem to motivate the hero's responses, the narrative discourse is above all spurred and sustained by the prospective absence of the protagonist.

Apparently stimulated by something present yet absent, the hero's desires and actions spring from the prospect of absence inherent in the conspicuous presence of the hero.

Typically obscured by presence the difference separating and associating presence and absence forms an intrinsic relational configuration underpinning the narrative discourse.

As observed in psychoanalytical models the experience of desire is intimately linked to "lack", and Silverman notes that "one could say of the Lacanian subject that it is almost entirely defined by lack" (151).

The presence of absence or lack is evident in so-called cinematic suture, in a relational interplay "largely synonymous with the operations of classic narrative, […] within which the values of absence and lack always play a central role" (214).

Particularly explicit in the classical tragedy the difference linking illustrious presence and a predictable death substantially enhances the dramatic energy.

In the Hollywood drama the presence of death is increasingly accentuated, and the narrative unfolding is further stimulated by the hero's struggles to remain present, to eliminate the prospect of absence embodied in the villains.

And to fulfil the promise suggested by something.

The hero's desires and goals are all recognizable as motivated by absence, as caused by characters capable of causing absence.

By objects and abstractions defining a promise of presence.

As much as actions prompted by something, the hero's reactions will also appear as provoked by the prospect of "nothingness".

The hero wants badly to remain present, and is having difficulty doing so.

Dancyger and Rush see a cinematic "premise" as "central to the screen story and best posited in terms of the central conflict for the main character" (2-3).

Egri more generally associates the premise with the basis for logical arguments and conclusions, and argues that "Every good play must have a well-formulated premise".

Within a wider context the premise is seen as "the motivating power behind everything we do", and related to the art of dramatic writing the premise should outline "a thumbnail synopsis" and include the character, the conflict and the conclusion(6-10).

To Egri the premise of a play is not always immediately obvious and may be difficult to define, even for the writer.

An ambiguous premise will tend to muddle the play, and while not necessarily entailing a universal truth the premise should suggest the direction of the discourse, and be identified and "argued" consistently, preferably in accordance with the writer's conviction.

Significantly, Egri observes that thousands of plays and playwrights can employ the same premise, as has happened throughout the histories of drama, and while the same premise may be expressed in an endless number of different plays, variations in the premise will always change the play.

A strong premise is seen to distinguish a good play.

At least persistently regenerated the Hollywood drama employs a standardized and uniform if transparent and somewhat deceptive premise.

The premise specifies the logic of the drama, and while Daniel's thumbnail synopsis seems to capture the theme or topic of the canonical story, it does not include the full scope of the classical premise.

The narrative conflict, accentuating the presence of absence, adds a significant aspect to the something desired by the hero.

In view of a recurrent threat of death and ultimate absence, the hero's desires will appear as an understatement.

Rather than actions motivated by desires for something, the hero's responses will gradually seem compelled by the presence of "nothingness". By a fundamental existential fear expressing the energy signalled by an always present prospect of subjective absence.

The term may seem exaggerated, particularly in relation to a celebrated cinematic hero, who may show signs of worry and alarm, but seldom angst or fear.

Whose angst is mainly expressed through seldom showing signs of angst.

While typically manifest in fears of poverty and lack of social recognition, in worries and distress related to the absence of love and money, the existential angst obscured by the hero's actions is based on a wider configuration of presence, difference and absence.

Explicitly linked to fears of death and "non-being", more explicit expressions of angst are recognizable in less moderate and socially restrained responses.

Whereas desires may stimulate passion, activity and even antagonism, only fear may "justify" and propel the violence and aggression repeatedly displayed by the cinematic hero.

While unfulfilled desires may give rise to frustration and distress, only angst and fear may produce fury to the point of self-destruction, and spur the extreme reactions adopted and accepted by the hero to counter, combat and eliminate any opposition, and all opponents.

Only a persistent if indefinite presence of consciously and unconsciously recognized existential anxieties, shared by heroes and anonymous readers/spectators, may sustain the self-deceptive processes of narrative regeneration.

The something repeatedly motivating the hero and justifying the narrative discourse includes an intrinsic if transparent fear of absence.

The premise persistently proposed by the Hollywood drama, the main idea the story is designed to convey, is essentially a promise of presence.

And all heroes' insistent desires to remain present are coupled with a generally shared difficulty, which is to reduce, alleviate and possibly eliminate a common fear of absence through continually redefining an illusory promise of presence.

Which always includes and accentuates the prospect of absence.

In terms of basic motivational features fear and desire will appear as complementary, and as stimulated and sustained by the same underlying configurations.

Where desire perhaps presents the more discussed and less controversial aspect. While fear and angst suggest and imply more obscure and less acceptable discursive forces.

At least in relation to Hollywood heroes.

Personified and objectified by antagonists and other forms of threat the presence of absence may appear as a difficulty which may be "removed" and resolved.

Once the threat of absence is convincingly eliminated, the promise of presence may seem to be fulfilled by way of financial wealth and subsequent sexual gratification.

With chaos imminent at the height of the narrative conflict, a balanced interplay and an improved state of affairs may eventually seem to be achieved.

To the extent, however, that something essentially includes the absence of fear, the problem repeatedly re-presented by the Hollywood drama is not resolved.

Absence is inevitably linked to presence, and all struggles to remain present invariably redefine and accentuate the prospect of absence.

As possibly eventually realized by cinematic stars and heroes.

Presence is inherently transient, and the presence of the hero, as well as the Hollywood drama, depends on a sustained discursive struggle.

At the end, the hero has indeed restored more or less the same states of affairs as at the beginning. Immediate conditions may have improved, but the prospect of absence still looms large in the background.

With respect to a basic and latent fear of absence, the cyclical play has brought little more than a brief and temporary, elusive and illusory diversion.

As flickering glimpses of light in the dark, as textual marks on a largely white page, observed from continually shifting perspectives, the hero and the narrative discourse cannot fulfil a promise of presence.

Symbolically, however, an illusory cinematic hero may to some extent illuminate the transient and deceptive nature of existential presence.

Milan Kundera argues that the novel does not investigate reality, and the novelist is neither historian nor prophet[36].

Instead, the sole task of the novel is to discover what only the novel can discover; the forgotten aspects of being, in a world reduced by science to an object of technical and material studies (13-16).

It is up to the novelist to draw the map of life and existence beyond a scientific horizon, to discover the different aspects inherent in the human potential.

And to investigate the role played by the irrational (71).

Further to the subjectivity recognized in most critical accounts, Kundera points to a frequently overlooked feature distinguishing a classical dramatic and novelistic experience.

The transparent experience of being.

Always incorporating a basic interplay of shifting subjective perspectives the process of narrative regeneration also postulates a conscious and unconscious awareness of subjective presence and existence.

Whereas the "subject" anticipates a cognitive dimension, the presence of "being" signals a bodily aspect.

According to Silverman "The term 'subject' designates a quite different semantic and ideological space from that indicated by the more familiar term 'individual'", and assists a conceptualization of "human

---

[36] Kundera 1987, 54-55.

reality as a construction, as the product of signifying activities which are both culturally specific and generally unconscious"[37].

Immersed in "the symbolic order" the Lacanian subject is "reduced to the status of a signifier in the field of the Other. It is defined by a linguistic structure which does not in any way address its being, but which determines its entire cultural existence" (166).

In opposition to the subject the individual, encompassing both a noun and a qualifying adjective, is employed to designate "an entity that is both autonomous and stable", understood to be a conscious and "free intellectual agent" (126).

Responding to this theoretical conceptualization Bordwell observes that "most [film] theorists conflate the category of the *subject* with that of the *individual*"[38].

The term "subject position" is seen to support the idea of the subject as an identifiable and individually distinguishable causal agent, "conceived as *the one who* knows and experiences", where the term has "encouraged most writers to treat the subject as an agent".

This tendency is reinforced by syntactic principles, as illustrated by Silverman's observation confirming that "the connections which are productive of meaning can only be made in the mind of the subject"[39].

Bordwell concludes that "At the theoretical level culturalists' conception of the subject have proven surprisingly 'Cartesian', or even pre-Cartesian".

---

[37] Silverman 1984, 126/130.
[38] Bordwell 1996, 14-15.
[39] Cited in ibid.

Resembling theologically defined distinctions separating the body and the soul, differences linking and separating the subject and the individual express the energies still maintaining an academic interplay.

Equally identified through a continuous play of linguistic regeneration the subject and the individual, like presence and discourse, will appear as complementary aspects in the sense that different descriptions of the same "object" may be equally valid even if they may seem to reciprocally exclude each other[40].

Employed by Niels Bohr to describe the nature of quantum mechanics the term suggests that a certain conceptual framework may preclude the simultaneous application of another which in a different context is equally necessary for the "elucidation" of the same phenomenon[41].

Adding to the problem, Bohr underlines "the relative meaning of every concept", which depends "upon our arbitrary choice of view point".

An epistemological problem follows from a relative subjective aspect inherent in manifestations of subatomic presence, where "no sharp separation between subject and object can be maintained, since the perceiving subject also belongs to our mental content". Thus, "a complete elucidation of one and the same object may require diverse points of view which defy a unique description" (96).

In order to illustrate the complementarity of different scientific views Richard Dawkins points to the so-called Necker Cube, to the manner in which two possible orientations of the same two-dimensional drawing may flip back and forth in consequence to corresponding shifts in the

---

[40] Risum 1993, 30-31.
[41] Bohr 1987, 10.

mental perspective, while "neither of the two perceptions of the cube is the correct or 'true' one"[42].

In addition, one may notice that a third meta-perspective is necessary to recognize and combine if not integrate the other two.

Inspired by Bohr Janne Risum describes the ambiguous theatrical performance in terms of a complementary relation "which creates theatricality precisely through its complementarity".

Through partly and temporarily suspending a sense of reality a theatrical performance opens up a figurative space, neither true nor false, which will seem to expand the same sense of reality.

Related to the study of language Saussure observes that "The object is not given in advance of the viewpoint; far from it. Rather, one might say that it is the viewpoint adopted which creates the object"[43].

Language is seen to include several complementary relations linking the psychological and the physiological, the individual and the social aspects, as well as the notion of language as both "an established system and an evolution".

While the study of language requires different analytical perspectives, "there is nothing to tell us in advance whether one of these ways of looking at it is prior or superior to any of the others".

Together with a frequently overlooked bodily aspect the experience of being points towards the complex dynamics of "organic" systems, while the subject signals a fundamental relativity and probability distinguishing a never fully present experiential reality.

---

[42] Dawkins 1982.
[43] Saussure 1993, 1ff.

One may notice in passing that the subject suggests a "self"-referential aspect within a self-generative organic interplay.

+ + +

Conditioned by a subjectively dependent experience of being, the narrative structure includes an interrelated bodily and biological aspect.

Essential to a cyclical narrative discourse the threat of ultimate absence is based on a common awareness of bodily presence, expressed through an individually centred struggle to remain present, which indicates a certain existential aspect distinguishing the canonical story.

Herman Tønnessen has coined the terms "geneotropic" and "crypto-geneotropic" to signal the prospect of genetic aspects conceivably conditioning cultural processes and practices. And how we may disastrously underestimate the extent to which biologically and genetically conditioned responses, rather than rational reflection, may influence how and why and what we find reasonable and right, logical and good.

Tønnessen finds it potentially fatal that language and linguistic signification, the medium through which we speak and think, may above all deserve a geneotropic, or rather a crypto-geneotropic label.

Since *The Origin of Species*, and again after Edward O. Wilson's *Sociobiology*, numerous studies have argued for and against theoretical models describing mental processes from biological and genetic points of view.

Among many, Barbara Ehrenreich and Janet McIntosh react to the "pseudo-biology", the media-supported "simplistic biological reductionism", and the "schlock genetics [that has] become the default explanation for every aspect of human behaviour"[44].

Arguing against "essentialist" models offered by "biologically based communalities that cut across cultural differences", they point towards "inclusive and complex thinking".

Towards processes of probabilistic genetic interaction.

Where Dawkins agrees that "It is perfectly possible to hold that genes exert a statistical influence on human behaviour while at the same time believing that this influence can be modified, overridden or reversed by other influences"[45].

Francis F. Steen, briefly reviewing Ehrenreich and McIntosh' paper, views cognition as a possible "missing link" between biology and culture, and welcomes the development of "a conceptual framework or blended space broad enough to handle both discourses"[46].

To Steen "cognition undeniably has a biological dimension", while Ehrenreich and McIntosh significantly observe that "There is no biology that is not culturally mediated".

+ + +

Linguistic signs, and figurative configurations of being, may be described as regenerative rather than reproductive manifestations.

Shaped by and sustaining continuous and cyclical but never quite identical discursive processes.

As unified and integrated structures, which embody and emerge as largely self-regulative systemic expressions.

---

[44] Ehrenreich 1997.
[45] Cited in Ehrenreich 1997.
[46] Steen 1997.

Where such systems do not signal obvious or ultimate causal features, whether cultural or biological, but rather include networks of regenerative relations, more or less identifiable as recurrent patterns and principles, which may be recognized and described in terms of a certain logic.

The recurring features distinguishing the classical Hollywood drama are conventionalized and maintained through the cyclical play of narrative regeneration.

As basic configurations sustaining and sustained by a canonical story. Which in turn is conditioned by centuries of ceaseless and often senseless struggle. By an individually centred existential interplay, mainly motivated by the threat of absence, and stimulated by a promise of presence.

As a recurrent figurative manifestation the canonical story embodies and expresses the paradoxical logic identified by centuries of irrational coexistence.

Whether or not these processes are conditioned if not determined by genetic features remains to be discussed and discovered.

While the integrated interplay of linguistic regeneration and narrative re-presentation may embrace an evolutionary aspect, genetic models have equally emerged through linguistically dependent processes, as culturally conditioned constructions within a broadly figurative and partly fictitious "symbolic" order.

Not necessarily including inherent genetic or "geneotropic" aspects, the regenerative logic distinguishing the narrative discourse may possibly inspire critical discussions of canonical stories as persistently renewing and reiterating "Darwinian" ideas, suggested and substantiated by centuries of irrational existential struggles.

In consequence of the overall relational complexity, the logic suggested by dynamic systems will be more or less simplified and incomplete.

More complex and extensive than immediately evident the span of relational networks embraced by the narrative discourse supports the regeneration of paradoxical yet productive, plausible but fanciful, stereotypical but never quite identical stories.

The logic identified by the stories supports a range of contradictory and essentially irrational discursive responses, which may seem natural and rational, but which consistently underpin a narrative discourse inescapably resting on concocted conflicts sustained and accentuated by discursively blind heroes.

Even the shortest and simplest story, however, includes an elementary conceptual framework defining a rudimentary experience of being.

Describing a fictional elsewhere, all canonical stories depend on and redefine the basic configurations sustaining a fictitious experiential presence.

All stories are somewhat "realistic", re-presenting the recurrent manifestations of an experiential "reality".

Identified by a conventionalized discursive interplay, an underlying and overriding, obscure yet obvious existential logic preserves the illusion of reality.

Substantiating a subject-centred relational framework, a "self"-referential discursive field, the narrative discourse includes and illustrated how a self-regulative interplay may shape and sustain the presence of illusions.

Assisted by a crucial discursive blindness, and accentuating a threat of absence, the narrative discourse repeatedly redefines a figurative rather than "natural" existential reality, distinguished by angst and ignorance, desire and aggression.

In one of the few discussions addressing literature and literary criticism from an evolutionary perspective Joseph Carroll argues that "the primary purpose of literature is to represent the subjective quality of experience"[47].

Literary works are thus seen to "reflect and articulate the vital motives and interests of human beings as living organisms".

In so far as "The most important biological concept is the relationship between the organism and its environment", Carroll refers to "character, setting, and plot" as the principal and "dramatic" elements of figurative structures.

Evolutionary models may hence provide "a sound rationale for adopting [these] basic categories [as] a means for extending our theoretical understanding of how these categories work within the total system of figurative relations" (131).

Not quite in accordance with evolutionary doctrines the hero embodies a basic regenerative unit, within a cyclical narrative process.

As a prominent figure preserving a paradoxical if "productive" interplay, at times resembling a Hobbesian *bellum omnium contra omnes*.

Seldom found among other species.

Activated by the presence of the hero the narrative discourse rests on and preserves an incessant and largely irrational struggle, to maintain the presence of the hero, in the face of a gradually more pronounced and probable prospect of absence.

---

[47] Carroll 1995, 3.

Viewed from the perspective of the hero the setting at the same time signals a prospect of absence as well as a promise of presence, with the threat of absence embodied in other characters, and objectified in a mostly urban and almost always US-American setting.

The existential background portrayed in the Hollywood drama is typically simplified and standardized to fit the narrative discourse, and justify the conflict.

While maintaining the presence of illusions.

Spurred by the threat of absence the hero struggles to remain present. Simultaneously, the hero's struggles predictably expand and escalate a predefined and mandatory conflict, which arouses the fears enhancing the violence and aggression sustaining and intensifying the conflict. As well as the narrative discourse.

Deeply conditioned by a promise of presence, the recurring conflict confronting the hero arises from a common competitive struggle, supported by a kind of logic shared by both heroes and villains, writers and spectators.

In accordance with this logic both heroes and villains struggle to acquire "something", and through the struggle they sustain the conflict as well as the logic.

Dependably, an integrated promise of presence and being, of "Being as *presence*"[48], serves to justify the conflict and motivate the discourse.

As indicated by "something", and in spite of an apparent goal, the hero's struggles may seem motivated by more than love or money. Or love of money.

---

[48] Derrida 1978, 110.

When someone wants "something", even badly, he or she will rarely risk their lives, or eliminate a number of others, to get it.

Significantly, the hero's overriding aim is gradually accentuated as an urge or drive to survive. Which still obscures an underlying existential angst.

Prompted by the prospect of absence the hero's responses paradoxically if predictably provoke a threat of ultimate absence.

Always discursively dependent the hero remains present only in consequence to a recurrent narrative discourse.

In consequence to a renewed narrative conflict and a recurring discursive struggle.

Embodying and illustrating conventionalized processes of subjective regeneration the hero is motivated by a discursively accentuated "lack".

Aggressively reacting rather than reflecting the hero redefines a discursively defined threat, through a competitive rather than cooperative struggle, for an inherently ephemeral if discursively accentuated promise of presence.

Shaped and substantiated by a conventionalized narrative logic the discourse describes and depends on a continuous struggle for presence, simplified and compressed into a violent battle of life and death.

Intensified to emphasize the roles of heroes. And villains.

Based on a dichotomized differentiation of heroes and villains the narrative conflict is further spurred by discursive responses supporting a narrative interplay which fuels the fear, as well as the level of aggression.

Which further fuels the fear.

Even in the sparsely populated Western the narrative discourse persistently re-presents a hero whose fears of showing signs of fear compel him to face almost certain death, in a final duel, before refuge is again sought outside the social setting.

At the other end of the scale a range of recurrent war-movies embrace a massive social conflict, unconvincingly defended and maintained as a battle for peace, and more plainly propelled by fear and an aggressive struggle for "power", as a paradoxical premise for survival.

+ + +

While plausible and productive the narrative discourse is inherently irrational.

A promise of presence is linked to illusory ideas, as manifest expressions of a common existential angst.

Usually objectified as money, a promise of presence embodied in symbols of power, will reliably appear as something desired by heroes and villains alike.

Mainly manifest and measured as money, power is re-presented as a motivational basis supporting the narrative conflict, where inherently inadequate monetary power fuels and fires insatiable desires, which in turn sustain the narrative interplay.

As complementary aspects of the same existential "energies", angst and desire rest on broadly the same configurations of subjectively re-cognized presence and absence.

Only expressed through "discursive" responses in the widest sense, the concept of "power", like logic, includes and integrates the mental energies identified by networks of difference.

The presence of power presupposes the prospect of absence, and the concept is only maintained through collective surrender to concocted configurations upheld by a largely "blind" and reflexive discursive interplay.

The interplay regenerating the presence of the hero simultaneously redefines a promise of presence, which invariably includes the presence of absence.

Through the struggles of heroes and villains, whose responses are motivated by a threat of absence, as well as signs of presence, the interplay is repeatedly and predictably brought to "the edge of chaos".

Justifying the conflict the logic suggested by the narrative discourse identifies a "disruptive" as well as a "gravitational" discursive momentum.

The threat as well as the promise are identified by the same logic, and only by way of the same logic may power be seen to eliminate the threat and sustain the presence.

By re-cognizing a threat of absence the hero redefines the power of "the Other", as well as a potential threat simultaneously embodied in renewed manifestations of objects and others.

In the Hollywood drama the solution to the hero's problems, and the ultimate resolution of the narrative conflict, includes eliminating others.

Yet killing villains does not eliminate an overall threat, or solve a conflict identified and maintained by discursive responses sustaining a ceaseless struggle.

For power and presence.

As an extension of the power of money the gun is inherently incapable of removing a discursively defined and dependent threat.

Unless the gun is pointed the other way.

As a regenerative manifestation the narrative structure embraces the conceptual and relational configurations supporting an integrated promise of presence and power.

Through a cyclical narrative discourse the hero redefines the logic sustaining the presence and power of the hero, as well as the presence and power of the Hollywood drama.

The power of the cinematic hero depends to a considerable degree on the presence of the "star", whose power in turn is expressed through a not insignificant level of idolatry, based on commonly re-cognized and discursively accentuated social and sexual, physical and financial differences.

Similar to classical Greek tragedies, the Hollywood drama depends on the presence of "elevated" heroes, however trivial, who all reiterate a tragic human flaw.

According to Michael Roemer "Every story is over before it begins. Their journey into the future – to which we gladly lend ourselves – is an illusion"[49].

All stories are precluded and the central character enjoys no freedom, as obliged to act, or rather react, to the preconditioning pressures of the story.

Roemer argues that "To act is effectively to submit", and "Every action is a reaction".

Reacting rather than reflecting the cinematic hero obligingly assists the telling of stories.

Responding in accordance with narrative principles the hero submits to the persuasive pressures of the story.

Supporting the discourse the story is maintained through discursive responses spurred by the logic, where every story includes and redefines an aspect of regenerative variation.

Redefined through the telling the logic expresses the regenerative energies embraced by the story.

+ + +

Through a predefined narrative unfolding a progressively more present threat of absence will predictably enhance a certain existential angst.

---

[49] Roemer 1995, 3.

Through a gradually more aggressive struggle, further urged by spatial and temporal compressions of a ceaseless discursive movement, the angst eventually justifies a violent battle. For survival.

In which death is brought to the focus of everyone's attention.

Based on studies of the Western Jane Tompkins described death as "west of everything", as an "ultimate price", and as what the hero strives to avoid[50].

Faced with the "ultimate test" the hero responds with violence rather than "Christian love", and the narrative unfolding reveals "men's fear of loosing their mastery, and hence their identity, both of which the Western tirelessly reinvents" (24).

The lonely Western hero is seen to embody "inner confusion" masked by outward silence; "Men would rather die than talk, because talking might bring up their own unprocessed pain or risk a dam burst that would undo the front of imperturbable superiority" (66-67).

Struggling to achieve something the cinematic hero strives to avoid something else.

Masked by desire, an unacceptable fear of absence is typically expressed through a generally recognizable effort to acquire and embody power, usually through acts of bravery.

Through the course of the narrative flow an always present prospect of ultimate absence is insistently accentuated as a controlling discursive device, repeatedly confirming the notion of a cultural and narrative tradition all but obsessed with death.

---

[50] Tompkins 1992, 24.

Catherine Russell refers to "the denial of death" as "a cornerstone of social institutions and practices"[51].

To Ernest Becker, "the idea of death, the fear of it, haunts the human animal like nothing else; it is a mainspring of human activity – activity designed largely to avoid the fatality of death, to overcome it by denying in some way that it is the final destiny for man"[52].

Becker discusses man's "heroism" as "first and foremost a reflex of the terror of death" (11), where a latent "urge to heroism" is disguised as a general struggle aimed at "piling up figures in a bank book" or having " a better home […] a bigger car, brighter children" (4).

Added to the fear of death, moreover, is the terror of self-analysis and of "admitting what one is doing to earn [one's] self-esteem". Instead, "a blind drivenness that burn people up" is expressed through "a screaming for glory as uncritical and reflexive as the howling of a dog" (6).

In "the more passive masses of mediocre men it is disguised as they humbly and complainingly follow out the roles that society provides for their heroics".

In spite of centuries of coexistence, and "heroism", a blind and reflexive existential struggle is regularly portrayed and re-presented in the Hollywood drama.

[51] Russell 1995, 8ff.
[52] Becker 1973, ix.

A recurring topic in all stories, an unbroken "heroic" struggle involves rivalling heroes and villains ceaselessly following out their roles, while screaming for glory through an uncritical and reflexive quest for power.

And presence.

+ + +

Responding blindly and reflexively to narrative imperatives the hero struggles, not primarily to survive, but equally importantly to alleviate the fears aroused by an aggressive struggle.

Assisted by the "reproductive fitness" of the star, by the power of the idol, the hero struggles to preserve the presence of the hero.

As well as the status of the star.

While preserving and perpetuating the narrative configurations supporting the angst substantiating the Hollywood drama.

And vice versa.

Maintained through the cyclical narrative discourse the presence of the hero stimulates a transparent practice of common discursive diversion.

Or distortion.

As observed by Becker a common denial of death may be recognized in terms of repression.

The terror of death is continually repressed to allow mental functioning, and Becker refers to Gregory Zilboorg who "points out that this fear is actually an expression of the instinct of self-preservation, which functions as a constant drive to maintain life and to master the dangers that threaten life" (16).

To Zilboorg "The very term 'self-preservation' implies an effort against some force of disintegration; the affective aspect of this is fear, fear of death"[53].

This fear of death arises from a conscious and unconscious awareness of what Becker describes as the "painful contradictions" of being, of being "out of nature and hopelessly in it", alive and destined to die. Which give rise to different yet interrelated responses ranging from belief in immortality, to degrees of "blind obliviousness" (26-27).

With reference to Pascal's reflection that "Men are so necessarily mad that not to be mad would amount to another form of madness"[54], Becker asserts that "everything that man does in his symbolic world is an attempt to deny and overcome his grotesque fate".

Forms of everyday activity may to the critical eye appear as "agreed madness, shared madness, disguised and dignified madness, but madness all the same".

Like Becker Tønnessen acknowledges the blessings of stupidity, also noticed by Wodehouse, to whom the only guarantee for lifelong happiness depends on being kicked in the head by a horse, preferably well before school age[55].

Stupidity involves and indicates a certain lack of common sense, and conscious reflection, whereas repression suggests unconscious restraints, and a potentially pathological aspect, with neuroses and "madness" as possible consequences.

Viewing the problem from a different set of perspectives Tønnessen refers to stupidity as an extreme state of "wellbeing", where

---

[53] Cited in Becker 1973, 16.
[54] Cited in ibid., 27.
[55] Tønnessen 1983, 44.

lesser degrees of folly may be balanced by more active and more or less conscious modes of distraction and diversion.

Tønnessen views a widespread and broadly uncritical acceptance of the reproductive cycle as linked to forms of practices and processes consciously and unconsciously aimed at "active wellbeing", in the face of a certain if indefinite death (42).

Death is tolerated as natural, and comfort is sought through activity, and through conceptualizations of absence as a form of presence.

Presence is continually re-constructed to mask the absence, and an inevitable process of dying, while always "painfully" present, is obscured by vigorous pursuits of pleasure and diversion, predominantly if paradoxically through work.

In combination with religious beliefs, and an equally ambiguous search for meaning.

As indicated by Peter W. Zapffe's distinction between "autotelic" and "heterotelic" activities, work may be seen as providing meaning in and by itself, often involving the blind drivenness described by Becker (48).

Further to more common forms of diversion, such as drugs and delusions, work and psychiatry, Tønnessen's rather unorthodox vocabulary illustrates and underlines how often "automatic" modes of diversion may serve to temporarily relieve some of the pain and anxiety aroused by the presence of absence.

While repression suggests a form of unconscious diversion, the practices and processes of actively masking the threat of absence include a range of conscious and unconscious responses.

In relation to more or less conscious discursive processes Tønnessen emphasizes "the over-credulous, unsuspecting praxis of our quotidian vernacular, our 'ordinary language'", together with the inconspicuous yet fundamental manner in which "our mode of thinking, feeling, perceiving, evaluating – in short; our form of life – is imbued and thoroughly saturated with a 'genetic' orientation"[56].

And, one might add, with a certain narrative tradition.

In addition to a biological dimension, and together with numerous other significant aspects, continuous and partly unconscious processes of linguistic regeneration depend on and sustain a comprehensive network of discursively conventionalized and consolidated fictional and figurative configurations.

Whereas the difference linking the signifier and the signified is arbitrary, it is also entirely discursively institutionalized, expressing a regenerative potential arising from collective acceptance and general "submission" to established configurations.

The play of linguistic regeneration and re-presentation rests to a considerable degree on common re-cognition of principles and rules which have emerged through the discourse, and which are consolidated through continuous and collective discursive practices.

In so far as the story conditions the telling, linguistic meaning will seem to control and constrain a regenerative linguistic practice.

As pointed out by Saussure's distinction between language and speech, the system broadly predefines the overall scope of the systemic interplay.

As illustrated by the Hollywood system stylistic conventions and narrative principles jointly support and restrain the cyclical discourse.

And inseparably linked to a stable if fluctuating subject, the discourse is decisively conditioned by systemic if simplified relational configurations, identified by a subject-centred experience of being.

---

[56] Tennessen 1983, 202ff.

An experience of being is identified by and included in an extensive relational framework sometimes referred to as a "symbolic" order, and described by Silverman as "the larger discursive field" (42).

Embracing a coherent system of referential interdependence a symbolic discursive field includes and integrates a complex of interrelated systemic attractors, which limit the scope of plausible and probable discursive responses.

And assist an unsuspicious praxis of ordinary regeneration.

Particularly conspicuous in the narrative discourse a set of conventionalized discursive principles, conditioned by a culturally specific symbolic order, will seem to support and redefine a particular kind of discursive field.

+ + +

Discussing the "shifted" interplay distinguishing connotative linguistic signs, Roland Barthes describes "myth" as a type of speech, as a system of communication and a particular mode of signification[57].

Supported by a "second-order" linguistic system, a kind of secondary language or metalanguage in which "one speaks about the first", mythical speech is seen to function "to distort, not to make disappear" (131).

Significantly, Barthes describes "the very principle of myth" as the transformation of "history into nature" (140).

Summing up his discussion of "dramatic logic", Keir Elam observes that "the drama can be understood as what Yuri Lotman terms 'a secondary

---

[57] Barthes 1973, 117ff.

modelling system' (others being literature, painting and man's cultural activities in general), founded on the primary system whereby man organizes and 'models' his world, namely language" (133).

A cyclical narrative interplay may be seen to include a form of figurative or mythical regeneration, assisted by language, through which a distorted discursive field is repeatedly redefined and more or less naturalized.

Conversely, the figurative configurations consolidated by narrative regeneration, will effectively condition and constrain the scope of the narrative discourse.

Persistently redefining a figurative discursive field the narrative discourse effectively sustains a particular kind of second-order discursive logic.

Seen as logical.

The presence of a figurative discursive field does not indicate or signal the prospect of a more objective or absolute existential realm, distorted by figurative rather than ordinary discursive regeneration.

Instead, the term suggests that an ordinary discursive practice, always conditioned and constrained by a discursively consolidated symbolic order, invariably redefines a more or less distorted experiential and existential space.

Even when measured by figurative standards.

Within an inherently mythical and figurative discursive field, the transparent presence of various aspects may signal and involve different levels of discursive awareness.

In so far as figurative abstractions depend on processes of intellectual reflection, the presence and renewal of mythical configurations depend on a more uncritical and partly blind discursive interplay.

While figurative models may be identified and corrected in consequence to critical investigations, myths are mainly maintained as convictions and beliefs, mostly in spite of being obviously flawed and fictitious.

In spite of being based on ancient stories. Of supernatural beings.

As a kind of second-order systemic space, a mythical discursive field will appear in consequence to more conscious discursive processes, involving different perspectives and a heightened level of linguistic and conceptual re-cognition and comprehension.

Critical explorations of mythical distortion will demand and depend on an expanded discursive interplay, less restrained by a conventionalized symbolic order, and involving a certain analytical awareness.

A practice of mythical distortion becomes apparent in narrative re-presentations of death as a threat. And in equally deceptive diversions of the threat.

According to Tønnessen language broadly fails to capture the nothingness of death, where metaphors suggesting forms of "Afterlife" may serve to mask the prospect of absence in terms of presence.

Instead of merely "mortal", which implies being capable of dying, Tønnessen points to human beings as essentially "*moribund* [...] *condemned* to death without any possibility of parole"[58]. From the moment of conception man may be considered "a budding corpse", and death may be seen as "a retroactive abortion". It becomes a gross if common exaggeration to claim to have saved a human life, when certain

---

[58] Tennessen 1983, 203.

death is only temporarily postponed, "for all the difference it makes" (35-36).

With such rough if reasonable examples Tønnessen draws attention to linguistic strategies adopted to divert an otherwise obvious presence of absence.

Although repeatedly accentuated, the presence of death is constantly and almost simultaneously veiled in linguistic and conceptual terms, as illustrated by the style and terminology used at burials, designed to comfort the bereaved, and shroud the presence of death with positive descriptions of a peaceful "beyond" (66).

After centuries of wars and violence, social rivalry and ceaseless struggles, encouraged by public executions and memorable depictions of Hell, all stories and Histories of human bestiality are vigorous and colourful, while accounts of a Christian paradise are strangely vague an unconvincing[59].

Offering to mask the threat of absence by way of narrative diversion and distortion, the Hollywood drama characteristically includes and accentuates the presence of death, as a precondition to apparently alleviating a discursively enhanced angst.

In the classical tragedy the hero is offered as a scapegoat whose often violent death, predictably evoking pity and fear, is presented to pacify a latent and thus aroused common angst, by way of a proxy.

Employed in religious rituals around the world, the strategy involves the sacrifice of glorified "heroes", whose sacrificial value is increased with an elevated social status, and whose death is offered to

---

[59] Bjørneboe 1982, 316.

divert a threat embodied in gods and objectified forces, believed to also embody a promise of survival and immortality[60].

Essential to the narrative discourse the angst aroused by a recurrent threat, of absence and death, is only temporarily allayed.

As suggested by an unbroken narrative tradition.

Contrived to justify the discourse the conflict is introduced to stimulate and motivate the angst, as a precondition for a concocted and contrived resolution.

By diverting rather than resolving the conflict, the discourse maintains and redefines the figurative configurations preserving the conflict, the angst and the discourse.

Further to the threat of death the discourse regenerates and consolidates a fictitious symbolic order, which effectively sustains a common existential angst, and a subsequent collective celebration of a ceaseless if irrational existential struggle.

Interestingly, Tompkins recalls that "Westerns made me want to work, they made me feel good about working, they gave me what I needed in order to work hard" (17).

Possibly in response to the blind and reflexive heroism suggested by everyday wage-slavery, the cinematic hero aggressively and violently struggles to earn the title.

Outside the Western the hero is frequently rewarded with financial fortunes far beyond any reasonable requirement as to sustained presence and being, as a commonly acknowledged sign of success.

And as a precondition for a subsequent re-cognition of the hero.

---

[60] See Frazer 1994.

In the words of Dudley Nichols "A story-teller is passionately interested in human beings and their endless conflicts with their fates, and he is filled with desire to make some intelligible arrangement out of the chaos of life"[61].

As other motivational aspects Nichols refers to "the desire to entertain", to "catch the imaginative faculties" of the mind, and to hold "the delighted attention of others".

In order to attend to the latter ambition, however, the storyteller has to contrive and concoct a string of narrative conflicts, which upon closer scrutiny may seem to depend on a decisive lack common comprehension, as to the "chaos" of life.

The presence of the storyteller rests on the story, and hence on a discursive interplay stimulated by figurative configurations regenerated through a kind of deceptive and delusive discourse.

Where the process of storytelling may illustrate a self-sustaining interplay.

Maintained by human beings.

Within a visual culture, in which man's aggressive and destructive struggles are ceaselessly made visible, a common and continuous practice of narrative diversion and distortion may seem rational and natural.

To anxious and fearful beings, daily confronted with visualized re-presentations of death and violence, suffering and misery, different

---

[61] Nichols 1943, xxxvii.

74

forms of subjective and collective distortion and diversion may appear imperative.

To Becker a common fear of death expresses a pervasive motivational force, a primary source of repression, which substantiates "recasting" psychoanalytical ideas traditionally associated with sexuality (25).

Within a human universe the presence of death forms a fundamental cultural and educational abstraction.

As demonstrated by the Christian cross.

Discussing "narrative mortality" in relation to "the discourse of death in narrative film", Russell observes that "Death remains feared, denied, and hidden, and yet images of death are a staple of the mass media" (1).

Russell refers to "the discourse of death" as well as to "an 'undoing' or 'reading' of the ideological tendency of death as closure", where both death and films are seen as "negotiations with absence; just as film is nothing but images, death is nothing except its various representations" (4).

Rather than a new cultural direction a more visual narrative interplay has come to accentuate the presence of death and destruction, aggression and fear.

Maybe too visual yet never completely present, discursively actualized yet obscured by the "semiotic thickness" perceived by Elam, the prospect of absence may seem to mask the contradictions sustaining illusory and deceptive appearances of presence.

Emerging through a continuous discursive interplay the presence of absence may seem more manifest, timeless and absolute than an inherently illusory promise of presence.

At best obscure yet always present, death has understandably if paradoxically become a threat, as something which may and must be avoided or diverted.

Typically through lifelong struggles for presence.

A common form of conventionalized "denial" is offered by an abundance of stories.

Yet only in consequence to a conscious and unconscious awareness of death as a threat, as something to be feared, may narrative diversion seem plausible and productive.

And only in relation to an individually centred struggle, for presence and power, in competition with everybody else, may a narrative interplay seem rational and natural.

+ + +

Complex, transparent and always incompletely re-cognized, all manifestations of presence are subjective and never identical, transient and never fully present.

As illustrated by a universe of "void", matter is all but solid, and the illusory nature of presence is repeatedly and effectively illustrated by the Hollywood film.

Emerging through twenty-four ephemeral images per second, the film performance is mainly made up of darkness, or absence.

Linguistic presence, embracing an interplay of difference set against a background of white emptiness, equally depends on a transient unfolding of shifting subjective perspectives, and discursive responses, conditioned by the presence of absence.

While writers may be more aware of the illusion of presence, most readers and spectators may seem oblivious to the contradictions sustaining the presence of illusions.

Common storytellers, as both writers and readers, readily recognizing and responding in accordance with simplistic stylistic principles, and primitive narrative conventions, actively and effectively assist and support a common process of narrative figuration.

Presupposing a certain level of conscious awareness, the play of narrative figuration assumes a considerable degree of unconscious discursive responses.

As vividly illustrated by the cinematic hero.

The cyclical process depends on and contributes to already established practices of subjective and collective diversion, which all rest on a limited scope of discursive responses.

Conscious responses beyond the level required to maintain the discourse will rapidly appear as unproductive or even counterproductive, and critical awareness as to the underlying logic, or lack of logic, will rapidly disrupt the play and distort the emerging presence.

The unquenchable vitality of a narrative tradition indicates, on the other hand, that critical discursive responses, threatening the process of diversion, may intensify the angst, and enhance a consequent desire for figurative presence.

Broadly irrational, "narrative" responses are conditioned and all but determined by the logic defined and sustained through the discourse.

Shaped by the recurring interplay the logic substantiates a range of blind discursive responses sustaining the cyclical process.

In so far as all forms of logic are man-made and simplified, and not including the full relational complexity involved, the logic prompting and justifying the narrative discourse is particularly primitive.

Faithfully following a predefined discursive pattern the hero illustrates a regenerative practice through which plausible and predictable discursive responses, seen as natural and normal, will seem to preclude the prospect of other discursive patterns, identifying other forms of logic.

Repeatedly regenerated, figurative presence embraces the logic as well as the cyclical process.

Rather than the effect of a cause the presence embodies both cause and effect.

As indicated by Tolstoy, underlying causal configurations may seem all but lost in a complex and continuous cyclical interplay.

Instead, a regenerative potential may appear as inherent in the relational networks defined by and underpinning the cyclical process, in the logic shaped by and sustaining the discourse, and in the lack of discursive awareness conditioned by and conditioning the process.

Masked by the figurative presence, and largely overlooked in consequence to an integrated linguistic and conceptual transparency, a vast network of regenerative configurations is partly recognizable in terms of grammar and logic, style and generic form.

$$+++$$

Illustrating the idea of absolute continuity of motion the Hollywood drama embraces a kind of complex causality which may seem to remain beyond our grasp.

Which may suggest that our notions of causality are simplified and flawed.

Rather than causal agents, heroes may be seen as objectified manifestations of a cyclical and regenerative interplay resting on repeatedly redefined configurations of presence, difference and absence.

The regeneration of figurative presence depends on discursive blindness as much as on intelligent responses, and on common recognition of relational configurations believed to be real and representational, absolute and natural.

Language plays a significant role, and through a largely self-regulative interplay a deeply simplified and fundamentally fallacious fictitious universe is repeatedly re-presented and made experientially manifest.

Perceived as representational rather than regenerative and cyclical, linguistic practices will redefine the grammar and the logic, the discursive principles as well as the relational structures, which at the same time stimulate and restrain the processes of linguistic and experiential regeneration.

A fictitious universe may hence be seen as a continually redefined manifestation of a largely self-sustained interplay, partly dependent on a sustained lack of common discursive attention.

The figurative configurations maintained by the narrative discourse may only evolve beyond the present primitive and primeval level through an expanded discursive interplay involving an expanded scope of intelligent discursive awareness.

+ + +

Presupposing a cognitive dimension, and a subjectively dependent existential awareness, the logic identified by narrative figuration may seem conditioned by centuries of blind existential struggles.

Also recognizable in classical dramas and ancient tragedies, a primitive narrative logic still supports a common form of collective self-deception.

While sustaining the self-destructive struggles offered by figurative "heroes".

Obscured by the killing of villains, and by highly improbably happy endings, a simplified and deceptive logic maintains a deeply distorted and destructive interplay.

From which only "heroes" may appear to escape.

Within a larger discursive field, partly beyond a figurative realm, the logic supports an all but equally primitive and primeval interplay, in which masses of "more mediocre men", and women, are urged to struggle to maintain collective processes of common coexistence.

Encouraged by forms of figurative diversion. And distortion.

By the telling of stories.

And the presence of "heroes".

References

Anderson, Joseph and Barbara Anderson. 1996. "The Case for an
    Ecological Metatheory". David Bordwell and Nöel Carroll. Eds.
    1996. *Post-theory; Reconstructing Film Studies*. Madison; U of
    Wisconsin P. 347-367.

Andrew, Dudley. 1984. *Concepts in Film Theory*. Oxford; Oxford UP.

Balázs, Béla. 1972. (1952). *Theory of the Film; Character and Growth of
    a New Art*. NY; Arno Press.

Barthes, Roland. 1973 (1957). *Mythologies*. London; Paladin.

Becker. Ernest. 1973. *The Denial of Death*. NY; The Free Press.

Bentley, Eric. Ed. 1992 (1968). *The Theory of the Modern Stage; An
    Introduction to Modern Theatre and Drama*. Harmondsworth;
    Penguin.

Bjørneboe, Jens. 1982 (1969). *Friheten. Kruttårnet. Stillhetens øyeblikk.*
    En romantrilogi. Oslo; Gyldendal.

Bohr, Niels. 1987 (1934). *Atomic Theory and the Description of Nature.*
    Vol. 1. *The Philosophical Writings of Niels Bohr*
    Woodbridge/Conn.; Ox Bow Press.

Bordwell, David. 1986. "Classical Hollywood Cinema; Narrational
    Principles and Procedures". Philip Rosen. Ed. *Narrative,
    Apparatus, Ideology; A Film Theory Reader*. NY; Columbia UP.
    17-34.

-       Janet Staiger and Kristin Thompson. 1994 (1985). *The Classical
    Hollywood Cinema; Film Style and Mode of Production to 1960.*
    London; Routledge.

\-   1996. "Contemporary Film Studies and the Vicissitudes of Grand
        Theory". David Bordwell and Nöel Carroll. Eds. 1996. *Post-
        Theory; Reconstructing Film Studies*. Madison; U of Wisconsin
        P. 3-36.

Brady, John. 1981. *The Craft of the Screenwriter; Interviews With Six
        Celebrated Screenwriters*. NY; Simon and Schuster.

Bukowsky, Charles. 1989. *Hollywood*. Santa Rosa; Black Sparrow Press.

Carroll, Joseph. 1995. *Evolution and Literary Theory*. Columbia; U of
        Missouri P.

Carroll, Nöel. 1996. "Prospects for Film Theory; A Personal
        Assessment". David Bordwell and Nöel Carroll. Eds. 1996.
        Post-Theory; Reconstructing Film Studies. Madison; U of
        Wisconsin P. 37-68.

Chatman, Seymour. 188 (1978). *Story and Discourse; Narrative
Structure
        in Fiction and Film*. Ithaca; Cornell UP.

Dancyger, Ken and Jeff Rush. 1995. *Alternative Scriptwriting*. Second
        Ed. Boston; Focal Press.

Dawkins, Richard. 1982. *The Extended Phenotype; The Gene as the Unit
        of Selection*. Oxford; W.H. Freeman.

Derrida, Jacques. 1978. "Structure, Sign and Play in the Discourse of the
        Human Sciences". David Lodge. Ed. 1993 (1988). *Modern
        Criticism and Theory. A Reader*. Harlow; Longman. 108-123.

Deutsch, David. 1988 (1997). *The Fabric of Reality*. London; Penguin.

Egri, Lajos. 1960 (1946). *The Art of Dramatic Writing; Its Basis in the
        Creative Interpretation of Human Motives*. NY; Simon and
        Schuster.

Ehrenreich, Barbara and Janet McIntosh. 1997. "The New Creationism;
        Biology Under Attack". *The Nation*. Internet;
        www.humanitas.ucsb. 02/26/98. 1-5.

Einstein, Albert. 2002 (1954). *Relativity; the Special and General Theory*. London; Routledge.

Elam, Keir. 1993 (1980). *The Semiotics of Theatre and Drama*. London; Routledge.

Esslin, Martin. 1991 (1961). *The Theatre of the Absurd*. Harmondsworth; Penguin.

Field, Syd. 1984 (1979). *Screenplay; The Foundations of Screenwriting*. NY; Dell.

Frazer, Sir James. 1994 (1993). *The Golden Bough; A Study in Magic and Religion*. Ware; Wordsworth Editions.

Frough, William. 1991. *The New Screenwriter Looks at the New Screenwriter*. LA; Silman-James P.

Fulton, A.R. 1985 (1980). "The Machine". Tino Balio. Ed. 1985 (1976). *The American FilmIndustry*. Revised Ed. Madison; U of Wisconsin P.

Furst, Lilian R. Ed. 1995 (1992). *Realism*. London; Longman.

Galbraith, John Kenneth. 1985 (1984). *The Anatomy of Power*. London; Corgi Books.

Garrett, George. 1967. "Don't Make Waves". John Harrington. Ed. 1977. *Film And/As Literature*. NJ; Prentice Hall. 105-??.

Gassner, John. 1943. "The Screenplay as Literature". John Gassner and Dudley Nichols. Eds. 1977 (1943). *Twenty Best Film Plays*. Vol. II. NY; Garland Publishing. vii-xxx.

Gleick, James. 1990 (1987). *Chaos; Making a New Science*. London; Cardinal.

Goertzel, Ben. 1994. *Chaotic Logic; Language, Thought and Reality from the Perspective of Complex Systems Science*. NY; Plenum P.

-      1995. "Cognitive Law of Motion.". Robin Robertson and Allan Combs. Eds. 1995. *Chaos Theory in Psychology and the Life Sciences*. NJ; Lawrence Erlbaum. 135-xxx.

84

Goldman, William. 1984. *Adventures in the Screen Trade; A Personal View of Hollywood and Screenwriting*. NY; Warner Books.

Gomery, Douglas. 1985. "US Film Exhibition; The Formation of a Big Business". Tino Balio. Ed. 1985 (1976). *The American Film Industry*. Revised Ed. Madison; U of Wisconsin P. 218-228.

- 1985A. "The Coming of Sound; Technological Change in the American Film Industry". Tino Balio. Ed. 1985 (1976). *The merican Film Industry*. Revised Ed. Madison; U of Wisconsin P. 229-251.

Gribben, John. 1999 (1995). *Schrödinger's Kittens; And the Search for Reality*. London; Phoenix.

Gruner, Rolf. 1995. *Not Proven; A Sceptical Look at Evolutionism and Darwinism*. Wigtown; G.C. Book Publishers.

Gunning, Tom. 1994. *D.W. Griffith and the Origins of American Narrative Film; The Early Years at Biograph*. Urbana; U of Illinois P.

Harrington, John. Ed. 1977. *Film And/As Literature*. NJ; Prentice-Hall.

Harvey, David. 1994 (1990). *The Condition of Postmodernity; An Enquiry into the Origins of Cultural Change*. Cambridge/MA; Blackwell.

Heath, Stephen. 1981. *Questions of Cinema*. Bloomington; Indiana UP.

Heuvel, Michael Vanden. 1994 (1991). *Performing Drama / Dramatizing Performance; Alternative Theatre and the Dramatic Text*. Ann Arbor; The U of Michigan P.

Hov, Live. 1993. "Om 'kunstgjenstanden teater'; Et teaterhistorisk gjenstandsproblem?". Live Hov. Ed. 1993. *Teatervitenskapelige Grunnlagsproblemer*. Oslo; U i Oslo. 54-69.

Howard, David and Edward Mabley. 1993. *The Tools of Screenwriting; A Writer's Guide to the Craft and Elements of a Screenplay*. NY; St. Martin's P.

85

Johnsen, Oliver A. 1978. *Scepticism and Cognitivism; A Study in the Foundations of Knowledge*. Berkeley; U of California P.

Jörgensen, Arne. 1992. *Vico; Myte, historie og erkendelse*. Århus; Slagmark.

Kennedy, Andrew K. 1983. *Dramatic Dialogue; The Duologue of Personal Encounter*. Cambridge; Cambridge U P.

Kundera, Milan. 1987. *Romankunsten*. Oslo; Aventura.

Lakoff, George. 1988. "Cognitive Semantics". Umberto Eco, Marco Santambrogio and Patricia Violi. Eds. 1988. *Meaning and Mental Representations*. Bloomington; Indiana UP. 119-154.

de Laurentis, Teresa and Stephen Heath. Eds. 1985 (1980). *The Cinematic Apparatus*. Basingstoke; Macmillan.

Lumsden, Charles J. and Edward O. Wilson. 1981. *Genes, Mind, and Culture; The Coevolutionary Process*. Cambridge/MA; Harvard UP.

Nichols, Dudley. 1943. "The Writer and the Film". John Gassner and Dudley Nichols. Eds. 1977 (1943). *Twenty Best Film Plays*. Vol. II. NY; Garland Publishing. xxxi-xl.

Pavis, Patrice. 1992. *Theatre at the Crossroads of Culture*. London; Routledge.

Pfister, Manfred. 1993 (1977). *The Theory and Analysis of Drama*. Cambridge; Cambridge UP.

Pinker, Steven. 1995 (1994). *The Language Instinct; The New Science of Language and Mind*. London; Penguin.

Reinelt, J.G. and J.R. Roach. 1995 (1992). *Critical Theory and Performance*. Ann Arbor; U of Michigan P

Richardson, Robert. 1973 (1969). *Literature and Film*. Bloomington; Indiana UP.

Risum, Janne. 1993. "Verden vil bedrages; At forske i at se på oppført fiktion". Live Hov. Ed. 1993. *Teatervitenskapelige Grunnlagsproblemer*. Oslo; U i Oslo. 24-43.

Roemer, Michael. 1995. *Telling Stories; Postmodernism and the Invalidation of the Traditional Narrative*. Lanham/Minn.; U of Minn. P.

Russell, Catherine. 1995. *Narrative Mortality; Death, Closure, and New Wave Cinemas*. Minneapolis/Minn.; U of Minn. P.

de Saussure, Ferdinand. 1983. "The Object of Study" and "Nature of the Linguistic Sign". David Lodge. Ed. 1993 (1988). *Modern Criticism and Theory. A Reader*. Harlow; Longman. 2-14.

Server, Lee. 1987. *Screenwriter; Words Become Pictures*. NJ; The Main Street P.

Sewall, Richard B. 1962 (1959). *The Vision of Tragedy*. New Haven; Yale UP.

Silverman, Kaja. 1984 (1983). *The Subject of Semiotics*. NY; Oxford UP.

Szondi, Peter. 1987 (1965). *The Theory of the Modern Drama*. Cambridge; Polity P.

Steen, Francis F. 1997. "Barbara Ehrenreich on Academic Antibiologism". Internet; www.humanitas.ucsb. 02/20/98. 1/1.

Sörensen, Björn. 1989. "Forfattere ved samlebåndet; Screenwriter-profesjonen i Hollywoodfilmens gullalder". Edda. Oslo; 1989. Nr.1. 34-50.

Tønnessen, Herman. 1983. *Jeg velger sannheten – en dialog mellom Peter Wessel Zapffe og Herman Tønnessen*. Oslo; Universitetsforlaget.

Tennessen, Herman. 1983A. "Language and the Dying of Death". *Methodology and Science*. Haarlem; 1983. Vol. 16. 199-210.

Tolstoy, Leo. 1982 (1957). *War and Peace*. London; Penguin.

Tompkins, Jane. 1992. *West of Everything; The Inner Life of Westerns*. NY; Oxford UP.

Varela, Francisco J. 1993 (1988). *Kognitionswissenschaft – Kognitionstechnik; Eine Skizze aktueller Perspektiven.* Frankfurt aM; Suhrkamp.

Wiingaard, Jytte. 1987. *Teatersemiotik*. Köbenhavn; Borgen.

- 1993. "Teatervidenskabens genstandsproblem og andre genstandsproblemer". Live Hov. Ed. 1993. *Teatervitenskapelige Grunnlagsproblemer*. Oslo; U i Oslo. 44-53.

Williams, Raymond. 1964 (1952). *Drama from Ibsen to Eliot*. Harmondsworth; Penguin.

- 1990 (1975). *Television; Technology and Cultural Form*. Ederyn Williams. Ed. London; Routledge.

- 1992 (1966). *Modern Tragedy*. London; Hogarth P.

Wilson, Edward O. 1978. *On Human Nature*. Cambridge/MA; Harvard UP.

- 1980 (1975). *Sociobiology; The Abridged Edition.* Cambridge/ MA; Harvard UP.

Winston, Douglas Garrett. 1973. *The Screenplay as Literature*. NJ; Associated U Presses.